I0487486

Online income secrets revealed:

revealed:

Blogging for cash

While every precaution has been taken in the preparation of this book, the publisher assumes no responsibility for errors or omissions, or for damages resulting from the use of the information contained herein.

BLOGGING FOR CASH - FIRST EDITION

First edition. May 1, 2017.

ISBN: 978-1393370420

Written by Andres Zamriver.

Introduction

How would you like to learn how to get paid quite a decent amount of money doing things that you love? This sounds pretty awesome, right? Wouldn't it be great to get compensated handsomely for doing things that you otherwise would gladly do for absolutely free?

This is exactly the kind of lifestyle many successful bloggers enjoy. Simply put, they get paid to write or collection information about stuff they're passionate about. You get paid to have fun. You get paid to live life to the fullest. Blogging for cash also enables you to turn your spare time into cash. Best of all, blogging produces passive income.

Unlike a job where you have to show up and work for eight-hour blocks of time, or else you don't get paid, if you blog for a living you can go away on a long trip and your blog will continue to make money even though you're not actively working on it. You only publish once and the income for that post continues to roll in. Sure, it may be a tiny income stream for each post, but if you have hundreds of posts on your blog, this can easily add up to quite a substantial and very welcome amount of cash.

This is the power of passive income. It totally liberates you from how most other people earn their money. Active income essentially forces you to live like a chicken. Do you know how a chicken makes its living? It has to scratch into the ground for it to get its food. If it doesn't scratch, it doesn't eat. This is why a job is spelled J-O-B. This is an acronym for Just Over Broke.

You're essentially just chasing your tail and trying to keep one step ahead of inflation. Unless you break into the ranks of upper management or you become a CEO, working for other people means you have to chase after promotions or try to get substantial pay raises. Otherwise, you're essentially going to be stuck trying to keep your head above water for a long, long time until you retire.

When you create a powerful passive income system through blogging, on the other hand, you create a system that enables you to earn money regardless of how much you work. You can be taking a long extended vacation with your family and you would still be earning.

This book teaches you how to blog for cash the right way. Just like with anything else in life, there's a right way and a wrong way to do this. Unfortunately, most people choose to blog the wrong way. This is why they fail. There are certain online income secretes involved in blogging for cash the right way.

The information herein is offered for informational purposes solely, and is universal as so. The presentation of the information is without contract or any type of guarantee assurance.

The trademarks that are used are without any consent, and the publication of the trademark is without permission or backing by the trademark owner. All trademarks and brands within this book are for clarifying purposes only and are the owned by the owners themselves, not affiliated with this document.

Chapter 1

Blogging for money: Separating hype from reality

There's just quite a bit of hype regarding blogging for money. After all, the concept of simply writing something once and making money continuously from a post you wrote a long time ago is very appealing.

Most people can recognize that they're stuck in a downward spiral if they're working at a typical job. They know that unless they get promoted consistently they will essentially be stuck in the same place until they retire. They're looking for something better. Not surprisingly, there are a lot of online marketing "gurus" who crank out all sorts of books that make all sorts of promises regarding blogging for money.

Sure, you can successfully turn your spare time into cash with blogging. That's indisputable, but there is so much hype surrounding blogging for money that it's almost become impossible to separate wishful thinking from cold hard reality. I'm not going to lie to you about the harsh realities of blogging for cash.

I'm telling you right now, if you fall for the hype, chances are very high that you will fail. The harsh reality regarding blogging is that the vast majority of bloggers flat out fail. How do we define failure? Very simple, they simply stop updating their blogs. According to the New York Times, around 95% of blogs that have ever been started eventually fail. They just stop updating and in the case of blogs that use their own domains, the domains end up expiring. That's how bad things are for most people who try their hand at blogging for money.

Another hard fact that you need to wrap your mind around is the reality that a lot of blogger who do end up making money from their blogs have to settle for chump change. They're getting traffic and they built a loyal community around their content, but they're not making all that much money. In fact, the overall commercial value of their online property is quite low. This is another harsh fact that you need to be aware of.

I don't mean to discourage you and I definitely don't mean of depress you. I just want to take the discussion away from wishful thinking into the realm of reality.

If you want to be successful as a blogger, you have to build your business plan on the solid foundation of reality. You have to pay close attention to these facts. You can't just build a successful blog based on how excited you feel right now. You can't build a successful business off the hopes and dreams you have regarding the success stories of big time bloggers. Your passion will eventually run out and you will eventually fail. It's too easy to play the game the exact same way as failed bloggers.

You can't just "build it and they will come"

The biggest problem many failed bloggers have is that they think the world automatically would demand the content that they create. On other words, if I'm excited about something, automatically assume that everybody else would be excited about that niche that I'm excited about. This is a serious problem because most bloggers fail to drive the traffic they need to successfully monetize their blogs because the demand simply isn't there.

Simply building something doesn't automatically mean that people will come to your online property. Traffic doesn't automatically follow. Sadly, these bloggers find out in the worst way possible regarding the number one rule of the internet.

The number one rule of making money online is: Traffic means money. If you're unable to drive up traffic to your blog, you're not going to make money. If you drive low-value traffic, you're not going to make much money. Do you see how this all works out?

Unfortunately, people who believe that they simply need to build a blog and automatically somehow or someway all this traffic will appear are simply just fooling themselves. They're just engaged in wishful thinking. I need you to completely understand this. Otherwise, you won't be able to build a successful blog.

In many cases, you have to make some painful trade-offs. As passionate as you may be regarding certain topics, there may come a point in your business analysis of your perspective blog where you have to let go of your top niche preferences to focus on a less preferred option.

The reality of contentment

Most bloggers are simply content to live on or look forward to a tiny fraction of the full potential their blog otherwise brings to the table. In short, they're simply settling for cents on the dollar. Also, I need you to be aware of this fact because the success tips that I'm going to outline in this book will help you overcome the natural tendency to take the path of least resistance. This is just polite way of saying that you're being lazy.

A lot of bloggers out there don't make the amount of money they should be making because they're simply lazy. They don't want to take the extra step. They don't want to look far ahead into the future. They'd rather just focus on the small trickle of chump change coming their way with the least amount of effort on their part.

If you are serious about blogging for money, you need to look at it as a business. You have to look at it as an activity that you invest the right amount of focus on to take it to its fullest potential. Otherwise, it's probably not worth your time. Otherwise, you probably would figure out that for the amount of money, time, and emotional effort you put into your blogging activities, you might be getting a better return doing something else.

Chapter 2

You have to blog smart to make money

As I've mentioned earlier, there are always two ways to do things in life. This applies across the board. You can choose to do things the smart way or you can choose to do things the hard way.

Choosing to do things the smart way is automatically doing things the easy way because – let's face it, if you choose to do things without the proper amount of information, it's very easy for you to make strategic mistakes down the road. It's very easy for you to make things unnecessarily hard on yourself. It's really crucial to be purposeful, systematic, and methodical in how you choose to lay out your blogging plan, so you can come out a winner at the end of the process.

Make no mistake about it; successful blogs do not occur by accident. I know a lot of big time bloggers out there like to play up the fact that they simply started their blog at the right place and at the right time, but don't let that fool you. The reason why those successful bloggers are still around and most their contemporaries are gone is the fact that they think in a systematic and methodical way. There is method to the madness.

Don't believe the hype that somebody's just born a successful business person or somebody's just born a successful marketer. It doesn't work that way.

Success is learned behavior. If other people can do it, you can do it too. You only need to decide to learn the right things. This book assumes that you can learn to be successful. This book is built on the solid foundation that anybody can learn to be successful by simply being systematic and methodical in their efforts to make money online.

Predictability versus Getting Lucky

A lot of successful people seem to owe their success to a tremendous amount of luck. It appears at first blush that they simply were at the right place at the right time. However, when you look at these lucky people, you'd realize that they owe their success less to luck and more to hard work.

As the old saying goes, "The harder I work, the luckier I get." You see, you can put a large number of people in the same place and at the same time, and give them the same opportunity as successful people, I will bet you that the vast majority of those people wouldn't know what to do with that opportunity. This is a key reality that you need to wrap your mind around.

You have to work hard for you to get lucky. The harder you work, the luckier you get because it takes a lot of preparation to turn opportunity into success. Don't let the seeming ease of the people who found themselves at the right place at the right time enjoy throw you off. They knew what to do with that opportunity.

You have to blog smart to make money. You have to have a smart process for you to predictably produce a desired level of success. You can't just bank on getting lucky. Mother Nature can throw you all the luck she has, but if you don't know what to do with that opportunity, you're going to continue to struggle.

Successful people are able to turn opportunities into success and they're able to do it in a predictable way. In many cases, they're able to turn adverse conditions into opportunities. Why? They have a system. They learned to know what to pay attention to in any given situation. They have an eye for detail and they're able to figure out how one set of actions lead to a particular set of outcomes.

Scalability versus "One-Shot Deals"

Have you ever noticed that they were people who made a lot of money at the stock market or in Silicon Valley, but after they established their name and made their money, they can't seem to achieve further success? These are called "one-shot winners". They simply were at the right place at the right time, and became big. However, after that point, regardless of what they try, nothing seems to work.

The reason for this is that a lot of their deals are one-shot deals. These deals just simply happened because all the right ingredients were present and things worked out. These people do not have the mindset to scale up their operation. This is why they're stuck with the memories of those one-shot deals. In the world of blogging, this reality also applies.

There are many bloggers who became really successful with one blog and once they settle that blog, and they try to start a new blog, those blogs almost always failed. In fact, I can tell you that the number of bloggers who were able to scale up and out onto a large network of blogs are very few.

In many cases, a lot of successful names in the blogging world cannot replicate their initial success. They're stuck with a brand that they established early on. The moment they sell that brand, they pretty much have an almost impossible time capitalizing on their earlier success. The reason for this is simple.

They don't have a systematic and methodical approach to their blogging business. This book teaches you how to create a blog system that enables you to achieve a predictable level of success. It also steps you through the process of putting together a system that would enable you to scale up your operations. Whether you are content with one blog that has a strong and loyal community around your content or you plan to build a network of related blogs, this book will enable you to put together a system to do so.

Similarly, by learning how to blog the smart way, you can create a system that you can replicate easily. Whenever you decide to sell your blog, its brand, and its good will, using the system that you created, you can easily create another blog and reasonably expect that it too would be successful. In fact, you should aim to develop a system where you're constantly creating websites and regardless of the fact that you're building and selling them, they would achieve a decent level of success.

You have to focus on being systematic and methodical. You have to have an overarching purpose in everything that you do. Otherwise, you're simply playing the blogging game to get lucky. Luck, unfortunately, can only take you so far.

Chapter 3

Pick your overall blogging business model

As I've mentioned earlier, you have to look at your blog as a business. It's not a hobby. It's not something that you do because you have spare time. It's not a personal diary. You're doing this to make money. You're doing this to put dollars in your bank account.

I need you to stay focused on this. Otherwise, it's too easy to blog whenever you feel like it. Unfortunately, that is not going to cut it. You're not going to be able to have the discipline that you need to put in the right amount of work to establish your blog on a solid footing. You can blog whenever you want based on however you feel later on once your blog has achieved traction. Up until that time, you need to commit to a consistent and predictable amount of effort as far as your time commitments are concerned. Otherwise, it's probably not going to work out.

Once again, to reiterate, you have to look at your blog as a business. If you're able to do that, then you need to focus on what business model you're going to pursue.

There are three common business models. I'm not saying that there are only three, but these are the most common. There are hybrid models that have elements of each model, but most of the business models out there can be reduced to three types. Pay attention to these business models because they impact how much money you can make, how much time you have to put in, and scalability.

You have to tie this into the amount of time, effort, and energy you wish to devote to your blogging business. Maybe you're looking for a short-term deal. Maybe you're looking for a business that you can pass on to your kids. Whatever the case may be, you have to tie in your long-term desires for your blog with the existing business models that may accommodate them.

Model #1: Build-Operate-Profit-Sell

This business model is very similar to a real estate developer. A developer would take a piece of land, build a home apartment complex or townhouse complex, and then quickly sell the property. They operate it long enough until it's ready to sell. Alternatively, they can build a property, rent it out so it generates steady revenue, and then eventually sell the property.

Regardless of which approach the developer took, the time frame for this model is relatively short compared to other models. Likewise, bloggers that use this model don't plan to own the blog forever. They simply build the blog, operate it until it generates a predictable and regular profit, and then they sell the blog.

The secret to this model is to operate it long enough to maximize its income potential. The key is to reach a point where you cannot get past a certain income level. Maybe you're stuck at $5,000 a month or maybe you hit a ceiling of $20,000 a month. Whatever the case may be, you operate your blog to its fullest potential and you hit an income ceiling.

By going through the process this way, you establish two things. First, you establish the full commercial potential of your blog business. You have demonstrated in no uncertain terms that this blog does make money, and it does in a regular and predictable way.

The second objective that you achieve is that you are establishing a pricing frame of reference for potential buyers. There is a robust marketplace for blogs on the internet. Sites like Flippa.com are used by blogger to buy and sell blogs.

One key element of blog sales is revenue history. Potential buyers will want to know the sustainable level of income of your blog. This is where they will base their valuation on. Typically, blog buyers would use a multiplier based on your average monthly income.

For example, if your blog generates $10,000 a month regularly, a buyer would use that monthly figure and multiply that by an industry multiplier. Typically, multipliers can range from a factor of 6, all the way to 24 months. Of course, the choice of multiplier depends on the niche your blog is focused on. It also depends on how stable its revenue base is.

Regardless, you have to be aware that there is a multiplier factor there and this should make it all the more necessary for you to operate your blog long enough to establish a stable income, with an eye towards eventual resale.

Model #2: Build/Operate/Profit/ Scale into one giant blog

I did not mean to give you the impression with Model #1 that most bloggers are essentially stuck with their blog once they reach a certain income level. The reality is, if you're willing to work hard enough and you have a solid plan, the sky is the limit as far as your potential income is concerned. In short, you will only earn as much as you are prepared to sacrifice for that income.

Keep this in mind because you can scale your blog into a giant brand. If you need an example for this, look up Copyblogger.com. Copyblogger started off as a typical blog that helps website owners write better website copy and blog content.

Eventually, Copyblogger turned into a giant media property. The same applies to Gawker.com. Gawker used to be a simple one-person blog, now it is a new media 'super brand.'

Make no mistake about it, your blog has the potential to become a giant media property. It all boils down to whether you're ready, willing, and able to put in the kind of work and capital needed to turn your blog into a powerhouse brand in its niche.

Model #2 is a very powerful business model because you can create a media property that is so powerful and lucrative that you can actually pass it on to your children. Entrepreneurs who subscribed to Model #2 usually don't think of building and selling their blogs. They're thinking of building it, so that it reaches its fullest potential.

Model #3: Build/Operate/Profit/ Scale into a network

Model #2 involves building up a single blog so it becomes as profitable and as big as it could get, however it remains solitary. You're just focused on one blog. Model #2 is actually great for people who cannot multitask.

If you'd rather keep all the things in your life simple, Model #2 fits you like a glove. However, if you are the type of person who would like to build a huge business empire that involves a wide range of different businesses and touches on many different subject categories, you might want to consider Model #3.

Model #3 is all about taking that one big blog and scaling it up into a network. Gawker.com started this way. Gawker started as one blog and then it started spawning different blog brands that specialized in other niches. Now, the Gawker blogger network is worth possibly hundreds of millions of dollars.

Make no mistake about it, if you want to adopt Model #3, you have to have a big vision for your network. You must also have built a very successful solitary blog that should have taught you all the lessons that you would need to scale into a network.

Chapter 4
Pick the RIGHT niche

As I have mentioned previously, one of the biggest reasons why many bloggers fail is the "build it and they will come" mindset. They think that if they have this hot idea that they think everybody would love and they build a blog around it, it will automatically become successful. I'm telling you right now. For every one person that gets it right using that strategy, tons of other bloggers just flat out fail. The obvious mistake in their thinking is that they're looking to build the business first and then find the traffic for it. Talk about making things unnecessarily harder on yourself. The better approach would be to pick the right niche by simply building your business around existing traffic.

Certain niches already have potential traffic. There's already a large demand base for that particular niche. You simple need to find where those people are, figure out what they need and put together your blog plan based on that existing niche demand. Doing things this way increases the likelihood that your blog will still be around several years from now.

I'm telling you, if you build a blog based on a hot idea with untested demand, it doesn't take long for you to completely give up. Why? Most people would give up after months of seeing very little traffic and, therefore, little income from all the hard work they put into their blog. Resist the temptation to build your blog around a hot idea. Regardless of how excited you are about your idea, at the very least you need to validate that first by looking for existing traffic. Is there existing traffic already? Is there proof and demand already for that particular niche?

In fact, I would take it one step further. I would focus on looking for a niche based on my passions but applying several filters that would ensure a market demand and commercial value. Here's how I do it. It is a systematic and methodical way to find niches.

What is a niche? A quick recap

What is a niche? A niche is a subject matter category for the cluster of needs, particular types of content answer. A niche is simply categorization system for types of content that people demand. People demand this content because they solve problems that they have. Niche selection is important because it can make or break your blog. It really is that simple.

If you pick the wrong niche, two things can happen. First, you might not get any traffic at all. Your blog is dead in the water because there is very little demand for that niche. The second outcome is you pick a niche that is so competitive that you get very little traffic. Sure, there is a tremendous amount of demand for that niche but your blog is one of millions of other blogs trying to meet that demand. Both these scenarios lead to the same place. They lead to potential failure.

You have to be very systematic and methodical regarding your niche selection. Ideally, you want to pick a niche that you're passionate about, has decent or very good commercial value and has enough traffic volume and with manageable levels of competition. This way, you can, at least, have a fighting chance in earning some decent money with your blog. If any of these factors are missing, things can get quite difficult for you. Pick your battles carefully.

By following the process below, you increase the likelihood that you would at least get a fighting chance at making money online with your blog.

A winning niche selection process you should use

Follow these steps so you can select niches for your blogs like a winner:

Step No. 1: Figure out what you're passionate about

Everybody's got passions. Everybody's excited about some sort of subject matter. Off the top of your head, type out all the topics that you're interested in. If you are drawing a blank or you don't know where to start, ask yourself this question: what kind of topics would I love to talk about even if I don't get paid to talk about them. Just write out first things that come to your mind. There is no right or wrong answer at this point. Just try to fill up the screen of your computer and just keep on typing whatever comes to mind.

As long as you are passionate enough about that particular subject matter or collection of topics that you would write and research on it for free, list them down.

Step No. 2: Filter your list based on commercial value

The next step is to take all the topics that you've listed out and go to Google keyword planner. Google keyword planner is a tool associated with Google adwords that gives you the rough commercial value of keywords related to those topics. Enter each topic one at a time and find the related keywords. Google keyword planner should give you a rough idea of how much each topic is worth based on how much advertisers would pay for clicks that show up for ads targeting keywords related to the topics you're interested in.

At this point, eliminate from your list keywords that have very little commercial value. If you're going to be targeting American traffic and in the United States, advertisers are paying very, very little for clicks on ads that appear for keywords related to some of the topics you've listed, delete those topics from your list.

Step No. 3: Filter based on traffic volume

At this stage, your list has gotten a little shorter. Now, you're going to look at Google keyword planner again, enter the remaining keywords and look at their traffic volume. Eliminate topics that have very, very little traffic. I'm talking about less than 500 searches per month. They're not worth pursuing.

Step No. 4: Filter by competition level

At this stage, you have a very short list of keywords. You're not done yet but we're almost there. Enter the remaining keywords into Google's main search engine and pay attention to the number of competing pages for that keyword. Eliminate topics that have too much competition. The fewer websites, the target keywords related to a topic, the better that topic is. At this stage, you should have filtered your initially long list into a very short list of possible niches for your blog.

This is extremely important to go through this process, because if you don't pay attention to commercial value, your level of personal passion, traffic volume and competition level, you might end up either competing in a very tough niche or chasing after ghost niches that really don't have any demand. You have to find a niche that has enough of these different elements for you to enjoy a reasonable chance of success.

Optional filter

Another filter you can apply on top of the other filters I'd just stepped you through is social media traction. You essentially take your keywords and search for them on social networks like Facebook or Twitter. What you're looking for are accounts or Facebook pages or groups that attract a lot of followers or members. This is an indication that there is decent to heavy levels of demand for the content that you are thinking of publishing. This is not mandatory but applying this filter would definitely make your job of driving traffic to your blog all that much easier.

Keep in mind that by looking for signs of high demand on social media this automatically means that there can be also high demand on other traffic sources like niche-specific forums and niche-specific blogs.

Chapter 5
Pick the right monetization model

Now that you have a clear idea of what you will be blogging about, the next end you have a preference for the business model that you will be using for your blog, the next step is to plan on how you're going to make money. You have think about this in a systematic and methodical way. You just can't say to yourself, "Well, I'm just going to put up adds." Well, you have to go deeper than that. There are different types of ads you can put on your blog, depending on your niche as well as the type of content you produce and how you engage with your blog visitors, some monetization models will make more sense than others.

In fact, if you pick the wrong monetization model, you are essentially guaranteeing the financial failure of your blog. At best, your blog would be earning cents on the dollar. At worse, you won't be making any money at all. That's how important picking the right monetization model is. This is no joke.

The key to optimal monetization model selection

The key concept to wrap your mind around when it comes to picking ways your blog will make money is the fact that different niches have different optimal monetization opportunities. Pay attention to the word "optimal." While almost all blogs can feature an Adsense, ad blocks, some niches perform better on Adsense while other niches do terribly. You have to focus on optimizing how you're going to make money off your blog. You don't want to put yourself in a situation where you trying to put a square peg into a round hole.

You can jam Adsense ads on your website. No problem there. However, be prepared to live with very little money. You would probably be better off if you had picked a different monetization model. It all boils down to your niche.

How do you determine the right monetization model?

This is where it gets tricky. You can take guesses but it is going to take a lot of time and a lot of lost opportunities for you to finally get a clear idea as to which monetization models work and don't work for your website. Your better approach would be to reverse engineer your competition. Regardless of what niche you're in, chances are very high somebody is already there before you.

Don't get sad about this. In fact, this should make you happy. Why? They're doing their homework for you. If they're featuring certain ads and you know that these blogs are the top blogs in your niche and they've been around for a while, you know at some level or other, their monetization model is working for them. Pay attention to the monetization models used by competing blogs in your niche. If you notice that a lot of them used Adsense, then chances are, Adsense should be your first option.

If you notice that a lot of them used CPA ads, then this may be the way to go. Regardless of how they make their money, pay attention to their monetization model. At the very least, this gives you a clear idea as to which monetization models to experiment with. This doesn't mean that you're going to stick with that particular way of making money but it's definitely much better than rolling the dice and taking shots in the dark and hoping to get lucky.

Reverse engineer

Do extensive research regarding competing blogs in your niche. Figure out on how they make their money. Use the same monetization model and then optimize your website's conversions once you're able to drum up significant traffic to your site. At least, you won't be starting off with zero ways to make money off your blog.

Common monetization options

I've listed down some common monetization models used by bloggers. This list is, by no means, an exhaustive list. There are a lot more ways you can make money off your blog. The reason why I'm listing down these common monetization models is that I want you to get a frame of reference. I want you to have a starting point. You can apply for these and put their ads on your website and then optimize based on how well your traffic works with these different ways of making money.

Clickbank

Clickbank is one of the Internet's largest affiliate networks for digital products. Unlike Amazon, all the products on Clickbank are digital. We're talking about books, software, wordpress plugins and other digital products. The great thing about Clickbank is that they are very liberal as to who they let into their program. Also, Clickbank is now available in a wide range of countries. If you're not based in the United States, there is a good chance that Clickbank might be available to you and you would be able to use Clickbank to earn dollars.

Clickbank is also tried and proven. It's been around for a long time. It's not a new kid on the block and it has a solid reputation among veteran and a newbie affiliate marketers alike. Its affiliate codes are very easy to work with. You can just copy and paste its affiliate links and hyperlink graphics or text on your blog to the Clickbank affiliate products you are promoting.

Another reason why I like Clickbank is the fact that it covers many niches. While Clickbank is most famous for online traffic generation products and make money online (MMOO) products, it actually covers a wide range of niches from making beer at home to natural remedies for certain physical conditions. Clickbank has a very broad niche coverage. This is very helpful for bloggers interested in a wide range of niches.

The big downside to Clickbank is they are very liberal with refunds. Let's face it, there are some people out there that would consciously buy digital product with the intention of asking for a refund and keeping the digital product. I just want to be completely transparent with you. You will always deal with this factor. Thankfully, Clickbank's refund rate is manageable but this can still harm you especially if you don't generate all that many Clickbank sales in a given month.

If you wish to use offers on Clickbank, pay attention to those offers' gravity score. While not a slam dunk indicator of success, gravity does shed some light on whether the offer can convert well. Keep in mind that different traffic sources as well as content strategies can lead to varying gravity scores. Always consider gravity score in context of how specific the offer is to your blog's niche.

Adsense

Adsense is the contextual ad system run by Google. Adsense automatically reads the text of your blog's posts and tries to display ads that are most related to the content featured on your pages. The theory is that if there is enough thematic similarity between the ads and your content, your visitors would be more likely to click on the ads.

The great thing about Adsense is that it has the widest niche coverage of all monetization options on the Internet. That is no small boast and it is quite an achievement. Regardless of the subject matter of our blog post, there is a chance that Adsense would find a direct advertiser or an advertiser that is targeting people who also would be interested in your content although there is no direct niche match.

Adsense is also great for getting ad retargeting clicks. When people go to an e-commerce website, and they go all the way to the check-out process but they don't do the final check out or pay to check out, Google would place a cookie on their browser. Whenever these visitors go to any web page that features Adsense ads, ads for that e-commerce or a service site the visitor went to will appear. In many cases, people would click the ad again because they've already shown a prior interest. This benefits you tremendously because you're essentially collecting when an earlier website did the heavy work of getting that person to click through to a commerce website.

The big drawback to Adsense is the fact that it doesn't pay evenly. If you get a tremendous amount of traffic from countries like the United States, the United Kingdom and Canada, you will get more per click. This is especially true if the niche that you are targeting has a high average pay-per-click rate. Now, if you are targeting a niche that has low commercial value and most of your traffic comes from developing countries or non-high paying countries, you will make very little from your traffic if you use Adsense.

In such a situation, you might be better off using a CPA ad program that caters to the country of origin of the vast majority of your traffic. Alternatively, you can try Clickbank. Pay attention to your niche and its commercial value with Adsense. If the paper-per-click value of the typical keywords associated with your niche is very low, I would suggest not making Adsense your ad platform of first resort. Try to experiment with Clickbank and the other monetization models that I've outlined here.

CPA offers

CPA stands for cost per acquisition. While that's a broad term that covers advertisers paying you for every sale their ads on our website generate, it also applies to lead collection. In most cases when people say that the phrase "CPA," they're usually referring to collecting emails or ZIP codes. Make no mistake about it. CPA ad programs can be quite lucrative because they require less work.

Unlike the typical affiliate offer program where you first have to drum up traffic to your website, then click an ad and once they get to a sales page, they would then have to whip out their credit cards and buy a product for you to make a commission, with CPA it's much easier. You only need to drum up traffic and when people see the CPA ad, they click through and there's showing a form. If they enter their email address or fill out a questionnaire or enter their ZIP code, you get paid. How awesome is that?

When it comes to relative ease, CPA ad programs are quite attractive. Now for the bad news. As you can probably retell, CPA programs don't cater to all traffic sources. If the vast majority of your traffic comes from a particular country where there's no CPA advertiser, you're out of luck. The good news is there are CPA advertisers for mobile-based international traffic. At this level, CPA would be your best choice if you get a tremendous amount of international traffic from otherwise low-paying countries. Just keep in mind that a lot of those CPA programs will pay only on mobile traffic

Amazon review sites

An Amazon review site is a website that features specific product niches or product categories from Amazon. You post reviews and pictures of the products along with an affiliate link on Amazon. The reason why I'm excited about this monetization model is due to the fact that the Amazon website is a very powerful sales platform. Once you get people to click on your Amazon affiliate link, Amazon will essentially move heaven and earth to try to convert that click. That's how powerful Amazon is.

Of course, it doesn't always succeed, but a clear signal of this heavy duty sales push by Amazon, is the ad retargeting that they do. For example, if you run a review blog that focuses on baby carriages featured by Amazon and somebody clicks on one of your affiliate links, they go to a product page on Amazon. If they do not buy right then and there, Amazon will place a cookie on their browser. The next time they go to Facebook or any other website, they will see an ad for the products that they were viewing at Amazon.

In many cases, people click through. Since Amazon ties the ad to your affiliate ID, there's a strong chance that you would get paid for that sale. Of course, this won't work if a person went to another Amazon review site after visiting yours, regardless you get more than one bite at the apple. How awesome is that?

Kindle book sales

Another way you can make money off your blog is to write a book on our niche specialty. When you run a blog, you are putting in a great position to know what people are interested in. In many cases, people ask all sorts of questions on your blog's comment section. If you pay attention to all these feedback and write a book answering the needs of your visitors, you can advertise that book on your blog.

This is a tremendous money-making opportunity because people already showing up to your blog with certain needs. They have certain problems that they're trying to solve. Since this self-published Kindle book speaks to their needs, there's a high chance that they would buy the book. Kindle may not make you an overnight millionaire if you write enough specialized books and you pop enough loyal traffic to your website, selling Kindle books can lead to a very decent passive income stream.

As I've mentioned earlier, use this initial monetization models suggestions as starting points. In the case of Clickbank and CPA programs, feel free to experiment with offers that are directly related to your niche or offers that people interested in our niche also historically prefer. However you want to play it, make sure you experiment. Keep running different offers and certain patterns should emerge. You'd be able to see whether certain sections of your blog make more money with Adsense while other sections would do better with reviews or Clickbank products. The more you experiment and the more you validate using your conversion results, the higher the likelihood that you will be able to maximize the value you get for each and every visitor to your blog. The name of the game in picking the right monetization model is to maximize the amount of money you get for each and every visitor to your blog.

Chapter 6

Investigate your niche before setting up your blog

By this point, you might be thinking while I've already done all the research that I need to do. After all, you have figured out the initial ways to make money with your blog, the niche that you will be targeting as well as your business model. You also have a clear idea that you are going to be systematic and methodical in putting together your blog strategy. It's too easy to think that you have everything you need to get going. Well, not so fast.

In this chapter, I'll step you through the process of making your competitors do your hard work for you. You see, regardless of which niche you're thinking of targeting with your blog, other people have already gone ahead of you. This is actually great news. You might feel discouraged because they beat you to the punch, but listen up. They're doing you a big favor because nobody starts at anything as an expert. It doesn't happen that way.

When people do something for the first time, chances are, they're going to make mistakes. This is why it's very valuable for you to learn from the strengths and weaknesses of players in your niche. Pay attention to the discussion below because if you use your existing niche competitors to do your homework, you are going to start out with the tremendous competitive advantage. You end up starting with all their strengths as well as working around their weaknesses without having to sacrifice time, effort and money like they did.

Pick site design models

The first way you can reverse engineer existing blogs in our niche is to pay attention to their wordpress themes or design layout. Look for the absolute leaders in your niche. Every niche always has a leader. How do you know? Well, one way to determine a niche leadership is to look at their estimated traffic. You can hire a virtual assistant to compile a large list of blogs in your niche. Next, instruct them to look up these blogs' Alexa site ranking information.

Alexa is a service run by Amazon, that gives online entrepreneurs rough estimates of the traffic ranking of most of the Internet's websites. Have your virtual assistant rank all the related blogs in your niche based on Alexa score. The next step is to instruct your virtual assistant to use tools like ahrefs.com or Majestic SEO to look for the back link volume of these listed blogs. You're looking for back link volume because this is an indirect reflection of how influential or connected these blogs may be in your niche. This is not a slam dunk but it's better than nothing.

If anything, it shows that a lot of third party websites are linking to these blogs. Putting these two factors together, you should get a rough estimation of which blogs to pay attention to. Of course, this is not a slam dunk but this is better than taking a blind guess. Look at the sites that you think are niche leaders and pay attention to the themes that they use. One handy tool that I use is whatwpthemeisthat.com. I just go to that website, type in the domain of the blog I want to reverse engineer and nine times out of 10 and usually, this tool would show me the name of the commercial theme the blog is using.

Now, be prepared for the relatively rare chance that the blog you're trying to reverse engineer is using a completely custom theme. It does happen. This is especially true for big time blogs. Regardless, you should have a clear idea as to the type of themes your competitors are using. If you look at enough competitors, you'd realize that there's a certain pattern emerging. There seems to be some sort of "industry standard" as far as theme and design goes. Pay attention to this industry standard.

You don't want to create a blog that looks so different from the typical look people interested in your niche are used to. By using a very weird design, you run the risk of losing your niche audience. Try to stay within the safe range of the industry standard, at least when you're just beginning your blog. Later on, once you establish a solid brand identity, then you can come up with a more daring look that better reflects your unique brand personality. However, at least in the beginning, you need to stay safely within the "industry standard" look of the blogs in your niche.

Reverse engineer content models

The next step is to go through the blog post of the top blogs in your niche. Again, you're looking for patterns. This time you looking for how they format their blog posts. Do they use video with their post or do they use image headers. You'd realize that in the case of content presentation, there is also "industry standard." Again, mirror your content as well as your wordpress theme and content layout based on these industry standards.

It's really important to stick with the industry standards at first. Later on, once you established a solid footing and develop a loyal community around your content, you can then start experimenting with a completely different look or completely different way of presenting your content.

Figure out your niche's content selection model

Different niches have different content selection model. By content selection model, I am referring to how they come up with their content. Most niches feature 100% original content. The blogger would have to write out original content. Other niches, however, allow for a tremendous amount of curation. Curation is where you take links to content created by other people and put them on your blog. That is your content. Either you post a short commentary or text snippets with that content or you just publish the link with a provocative headline. It all depends on the industry standard for the content selection model in your niche. Keep in mind that most niches do have a specific content selection model. Pay attention to this. Your either dealing with all-original content, mostly curation or a combination of both of these models.

By doing a heavy reverse engineering, you make your competitors do your homework for you. You don't start the game trying to come up with a completely new implementation that nobody's seen before. That is almost always a sure recipe for disaster if you don't know what you're doing. It's much better to build your blog initially on the solid foundation of the solutions tried and proven by your competitors. By building on their strengths and avoiding their weaknesses when you begin, you can quickly gain a competitive advantage.

Chapter 7

Outsource the details and focus on the Big Idea

Now, if you've reaching this chapter thinking that you're going to have to do everything on your own, I have good news for you. The good news is you don't have to do it. In fact, thanks to the modern day miracle of outsourcing, you can pretty much outsource all the work that goes into your blog.

If you think about it, a lot of the big blogs and established brands in your niche are probably not handled by only one person. In fact, the typical life cycle of a successful blog is the blogger would first do everything on their own, and then reach a certain level of success. At that point, the person would then start outsourcing in chunks the different processes that go into producing the content as well the traffic for his or her blog.

Eventually, really big blog brands like Gawker.com are handled like any other corporation. The blogger simply assumes the role of editor in chief and pretty much delegates everything else. Of course, I'd love for you to reach the level of success Gawker has achieved. The best way to get there is to reverse engineer their success.

By having an open mind to quality outsourcing in the beginning, you increase the likelihood that your blog would be a success sooner rather than later. You have to remember that you only have one job. You might think that your job is to find pictures for your blog posts, find ideas, right content, promote, and so on and so forth. You'd be absolutely wrong. That's grunt work.

Your job is to look at the big idea behind your blog. That's it. That is your job. The sooner you are clear on this idea, the better it will be for you. You have to remember that people are not going to go to your blog just because you wrote it. They're looking for a brand identity. They're looking for a point of distinction.

If you're able to focus on this and outsource everything else, you increase the likelihood that your blog will stand out. If your blog stands out from the competition, there is a stronger chance that your blog will be successful. This won't happen if you don't have a clear idea of what your job is.

Your job is not to get lost in the grunt work. Your job is not to run around in circles. You can hire people to do that. Your job is to focus on the big idea, clearly define it, fine-tune it, and take it to the next level. That is how you can tell a blog that's going places from a blog that is simply a glorified hobby. It's up to you to decide which direction to take.

If you're serious about becoming a successful blogger, you need to accept the idea that you would have to outsource parts of the production process.

What can you outsource?

Well, the answer to the question that I posed here is simple: Everything. That's right. You can outsource pretty much all the different elements that go into your blog. It's a good idea to outsource the right way. As I've mentioned earlier, there are always two ways to do things. You can do things the right and easy way or you can do things the wrong and hard way. Sadly, most bloggers choose the latter approach.

Pay attention to the elements that you need to outsource, as well as the discussion on how to outsource like a champ mentioned below.

Outsource your blog header

Every blog has a header. This is the graphical or text element at the top. A lot of people confuse this for the logo, but their two totally different things. While a blog header can incorporate your logo, a blog header pretty much stands on its own.

It has different elements in it. Maybe it would have a slogan. Maybe there would be graphic that appears with the header. Whatever the case is, a blog header can be text or graphical elements at the top of your blog. You can outsource this to freelance graphic artists who specialize in blog headers. The more specialized the person is in your niche, the higher the likelihood that that person would do a great job.

What are you looking for in great outsourced blog headers? Very simple, you're looking for a header that captures the values that you want your brand's graphics to communicate.

Outsource your logo design

A logo is a graphical representation of your brand. You need to sit down and write down the kind of values you want your blog visitors to associate with your blog. Once you have a clear idea of what these brand values are, you can then run a contest on 99designs.com or some other graphic design platform to get professional graphic designers to produce logo designs for you.

The great thing about running a design contest is you're not stuck with one designer. If that designer produces a crappy design, then you're stuck. With the contest, you can keep the contest going until somebody comes up with a design you're happy with.

Outsource your theme modification or custom theme design

As I've mentioned in a previous chapter, you can reverse engineer the theme of your competitors. By simply using the tool that I've mentioned, you can find out the theme that they are using. Of course, I don't recommend that you use the theme that your competitors are using straight out of the box.

You have to customize your theme. While certain elements of your layout may look like your competitor's because you're following an "industry standard", you have to hire freelancers to customize the theme, so that your brand values permeate your site. People can still tell that used a similar theme as your competitors, but your blog is different enough for it to assume a personality of its own.

Outsource content creation

There are many gifted writers from countries outside the United States that have a large of population of people who speak English as a second language. I am of course talking about places like India, Philippines, Pakistan, Kenya, and others.

The great thing about freelancers that come from these countries is that they produce high-quality English texts at a fraction of the rates charged by American or British writers. Most of them are open to instructions, so as long as you invest enough time in walking them through the process of producing content that you will be happy with, investing in an outsourced company or a freelance writer from a developing country can a worthwhile use of your time.

You have to be clear regarding your content parameters. Don't expect your outsource writers to read your mind. You have to have a solid content production brief that steps them through the process of researching materials, coming up with topics, and writing and formatting the material in such a way that it would do well on your blog.

If they produce crappy content, nine times out of ten, it's not their fault. Usually, the reason why bad content is produced by an otherwise highly-competent outsource writer is because the client simply dropped the ball as far as instructions are concerned.

You should create a quality control checklist and put together a content production process. This way, there will be no nasty surprises down the road for either you or your writing contractor.

Outsource content curation correctly

Content curation, believe it or not, can be trickier than flat out hiring a freelancer to write your content. This might seem crazy to you because curation is simply just taking existing content produced by third part websites and putting them on your blog. How hard can it be?

Well, the short answer is: Very. You have to remember that the key to content curation is effective editorial analysis and selection. You can't just tell a virtual assistant to run a keyword search on Google News and pick the first few items that appear for the search query. You're going to destroy your blog that way.

They have to read through dozens of possible content selections and come up with content that would be of tremendous value to your blog visitors. This means that they have to develop a knack for determining what types of stories your existing user base or niche audience would be interested in. This takes quite a bit of analysis and this definitely takes time.

Don't think that outsourcing content curation is a cake walk. You have to spell out the selection process in fine detail. Otherwise, it's very easy for the freelancer to mess up.

I strongly suggest that you use a video and view going through the content curation process yourself, so your freelancer would have a clear idea of the analytical process you go through to determine a piece of niche-specific content is good enough for your blog or not.

Another key part of content curation is coming up with titles. You need to pick a virtual assistant who is also a very good writer. Otherwise, this is not going to work. Great titles are all about creating pictures in the mind of the reader. These are so effective that they do this very quickly. Also, great titles have emotional triggers that basically bait the reader to click on the title. That's how powerful expert curation skills are.

You need to be very selective in picking your virtual assistant because not all people who are good at picking niche content for curation can also do a good job with writing highly-effect titles.

Outsource your social media profile's set up

Setting up a social media profile is pretty straightforward. It is a lot of grunt work. You would do well to outsource this part. The other part of this is making sure that all your social media accounts have different, but somewhat similar, looks.

This way, when people go to your Instagram account, they can tell that the logo is the same as your blog, but there's enough difference in your presence that you can draw traffic from Instagram and pump it to your blog. The same goes with your Facebook page, Facebook groups, Twitter account, and other social media accounts.

The strategy here is to set up as many different social media accounts as possible and make sure that your covers there are similar enough to your blog, but different enough so as to maximize those different social media platforms' native traffic base.

Get outsourced help for social media outreach

One of the best ways to drive traffic to your blog posts is through social media. If you engage with the right people, for example, on Twitter, don't be surprised to get a massive blast of traffic because you got the attention of somebody who is influential in your niche. The same applies to Facebook and other social media platforms like YouTube.

To get this going you need to reach out to these people. You need to figure out who they are and engage them. The good news is you can outsource this as well. There are many competent and capable social media outreach specialists from place like the Philippines that can help you maintain a professional image on social media platforms without burning a hole through your pocket.

Outsource your guest blogging and other content marketing

If you are serious about driving high quality authoritative traffic to your blog, you need to engage in guest blogging. By using outsourcing you can reduce the costs of guest blogging. Make no mistake about it, guest blogging can get quite costly, but thanks to outsourcing you can keep your costs manageable by having a professional guest blogger establish relationships with other blogs in your niche and create backlinks to your website using high quality content published on these related blogs.

How to outsource like a champ

If you want to outsource correctly, you need to make sure that you train your freelance help. They may talk a big game about having done what you want them to do hundreds, if not thousands, of times before. It's okay to believe them, but you need to make it known to them that you want things done your way. If they want to do business with you, they have do things your way. This is how you outsource like a champ.

You insist that they do things your way. To make things easier for them, you have to give them a production sheet that spells out in clear terms how you want something done. You also provide them with videos where they watch you create a piece of content, promote that content, and do other tasks. This way, there's no guesswork involved. They can easily review the video, so they don't have to bother you with an email. They don't have to call you via Skype to pick your brain. They already have a video that they can refer to.

Also, you need to provide a quality control sheet. This is a checklist that you create for your freelance helpers, so they can have a clear idea whether they did the job right. They have to go through the checklist and check all items to ensure that they produced materials you will be happy with.

If you follow these tips, you will outsource like a champ and chance are quite high that you will encounter less headaches down the road. Headaches are inevitable. Whenever you hire somebody, there will always be an opportunity for misunderstanding. Miscommunication is not going to go away, but by following my tips you'll increase the likelihood that there would be less headaches for you when you outsource.

Chapter 8

Creating killer content: Focus on what already works!

If you're serious about becoming a successful blogger, let me clue you in on the secret to great content. The secret to great content is not coming up with completely new content. In fact, that can be disastrous. You will be engaging in the classic blogger mistake of, "Build it and they will come." As I've mentioned in a previous chapter, that strategy rarely works. Ditch that strategy.

You need to focus on what already works. You need to look at the content topics your competitors are already focusing on and pay attention to their reception. How are the topics that they cover being received by their target audience members?

This should clue you in on hot topics. How do you figure this out? Very simple, just look at the number of comments on that blog post and also look at the number of backlinks being generated by that blog post.

When people link to a particular post, they're obviously paying attention to what's going on in that blog post. The subject matter of that blog post is important to them. You can use handy tools like Ahrefs.com or Majestic SEO to determine backlink footprints.

Regardless of how you do it, you need to figure out which of your competitors' content is popular. Another way to figure this out is to look at the number of shares or the number of likes on Facebook.

Once you've identified that there are certain hot topics in your niche by looking at your competitors' content, the next step is to reverse engineer that. How do you do this? Very simple, you just focus on the same hot topics. It really is that basic.

Now, don't get me wrong. I'm not saying that you should talk about those hot topics in the exact same way as your competitors. If you do it that way, you are going to fail. Why? There's really no incentive for your target audience members to visit your blog when other more established blogs in your niche are already taking that particular spin.

They're already talking about those hot topics in the same exact way. Why should your target visitors go to you instead of those more established brands?

You have to do something different. You have to add your own spin. You have to focus on emphasizing your personality. Maybe you can find a controversial angle to the story. Maybe you can find a dissenting or controversial opinion. Whatever the case may be, you need to come up with your own spin to the hot topics in your niche. This way, you kill two birds with one stone.

First, you draw people who are interested in proven subject matter. These people are already looking for these hot topics. There is already demand there. Second, you differentiate your brand. You give those people a reason for going to you instead of your competitors. By taking a different spin, you give them something that they are probably not going to get elsewhere. You give them a reason to check out your blog.

Focus on what makes your blog different

If you consistently and constantly take hot topics in your niche and put your own personality and spin on those topics, you will make your blog look different. Eventually, a community of loyal readers will form around your content. Now, don't get too excited.

You have to remember that there will always people that will be mad at you. For some or reason or other, you just rub them the wrong way. Be prepared to let those people go. You can never please those people. Whatever your spin is, it's just going to rub them the wrong way. They're not going to agree with you.

The good news is that there will be a segment of people that like your take. These are people that share your spin on the hot topics. These are the people that you will build your content community on.

By cultivating this community, you create a loyal base of readers around your content, which leads to a distinct blog persona.

Create a distinct blog persona and brand identity

It's too easy to look at blog persona and brand as essentially graphical in nature. Believe it or not, there are lots of bloggers out there that think that their blog stands out from their competitors because they blog has a different header and it uses a different logo. This is completely wrong.

A blog persona and a brand identity involve values. When people go to your blog and read your posts, they develop an emotional reaction. These emotions are not neutral. They are tied to certain values. This is how you create a distinct blog persona and brand identity.

When people go to your website and they get a distinct emotional reaction which they can then identify with the values of your blog, you have achieved in standing out from the rest of your competition. This is crucial because most of your competitors are bland, generic, or clones of each other. There are a few giant brands in any niche.

Work hard to make your blog of them. How do you do this? Establish a distinctive blog persona and brand identity. This is based on quality content with a loyal community of readers cultivated around it.

Interlink like crazy

Another key to creating killer content besides focusing on hot topics and putting your own branded twist on it is to interlink like crazy. When you post content, make sure that there are relevant links to previous posts. The reason why you're doing this is because you want to get many bites at the apple.

What I mean by this is, when somebody is impressed by your content, they can easily click on a link and look at other pieces of content that you've written in the past. If they're impressed with those, they can click again and they go deeper and deeper into your website.

Not only does this increase chances that they would click on an ad and possibly buy which would put money in your pocket, but you're also getting something else of value. When people click through your blog and simply dig deeper and deeper into the guts of your blog, you are branding that person. There's a high likelihood that that person will associate you with certain needs that he or she has.

If interlink enough and you post high quality content, chances are good that this person will bookmark your blog, come back and become a part of your loyal community. It takes a while to cultivate a loyal community of readers around your content. However slow it may be, it is definitely worth doing.

If you have a loyal community of readers, your baseline traffic increases over time. Also, you get a loyal army of potential promoters that can share your content on their social media accounts. Simply put, you can turn your existing readers into your blog's cheerleaders.

Make sure you add as much value into each post

You might think that all the value that goes into your post is in the text. In most cases, you're absolutely correct, but if you want to be a successful blogger, you need to go beyond the call of duty. Look for related info graphics produced by third parties that relate to your topic. Look for related images or YouTube videos.

Whatever the case is, try to add to your blog post by adding content produced by others. Make sure that you put a short commentary with a link back to the source of that third party content. This way, you are free and clear of copyright infringement issues.

Copyright law allows for "fair use". Since you are featuring somebody else's work to post short reviews or analysis of that work, your content will fall into the realm of fair use. Also, by providing a link to the source of the third party content, you in effect "pay them" for using their content. They benefit by getting potential traffic from your blog post. This way, you create a potential win-win situation.

Still, if the creator of the content that you're featuring with your blog post objects, be ready to take off their content.

Chapter 9
Drive traffic like a champ

You have to know how to drive traffic for you to make money off your blog. I'm sorry to say this, but even if your blog features the best content on the planet, if there's nobody reading that content, you're just wasting your time. You're not going to make any money. It really is that basic.

The iron law of the internet is simple: Traffic means the opportunity to make money. Without traffic, you have to opportunity to make money. It really is that simple. It's really imperative for you to know how to drive traffic like a champ.

Interestingly enough, the starting point is not you rushing off to free sources of traffic of buying traffic from AdWords or Facebook. Your starting point is actually your content.

Focus more on promoting content instead of daily updates

You need to make sure that you focus more on promoting your content instead of spending almost all your time creating new content. This is one of the most common reasons why most blogger fail. They spend so much of their time posting materials on their blog, thinking that the more they update the more traffic they will get from the internet. It doesn't work that way.

You see, Google and other search engines have changed dramatically over the past few years. While you could get away with updating frequently to get traffic 10 years ago, it doesn't work now. It will not work in the future either. You have to budget the vast majority of your time promoting your content. Focus less on updates and focus more on promotions.

Now, don't get me wrong. Certain niches require daily updates. For example, if your niche is Stock News, then you need to do daily updates because that's what your visitors expect from you. However, if your blog is an Amazon product review blog, then you can get away with posting reviews every few weeks or once a month.

Depending on your niche, try to focus more on promoting your content instead of daily updates. It all begins with your content policy.

Drive traffic the smart way

It's very easy to chase your tail and run around in circles when it comes to driving free traffic to your blog. It really is. Many bloggers would create a massive list of all the places they can advertise their blog posts for free. They would then hit that list day in, day out. They keep at it for weeks. At the end of the process, they have very little to show for all that time and effort. Talk about a letdown.

If you don't want that to happen of you, you need to drive traffic the smart way. While it's a good idea to come up with a long list of places that you're going to hit for traffic, you need to approach them the right way. You need to come up with content that is especially positioned and crafted to maximize traffic from those sources.

If you're simply just going to spam that long list of traffic sources with a generic link, you might as well not even try. Your chances of getting banned or your brand suffering irreparable harm are too high. Focus instead on driving traffic the smart way.

Follow the strategies listed below.

Start with blog commenting

A lot of people have completely dismissed blog commenting as a way to drive traffic. In their minds, they think that blog commenting for traffic simply involves running a piece of software and blasting thousands, if not hundreds of thousands, of blogs with generic comments. I agree with those people if that's what you're going to do as far as blog commenting is concerned. That is no way to market through blog comments. I have something else entirely in mind.

First, you need to look for blogs that are tightly related to your niche. They have to be as close to your niche as possible. If at all, look only for blogs that are in the exact same niche as yours. Unfortunately, given how niches are, this is usually not the case, so look for blogs that have a tight fit with your niche. They have to be closely related.

Next, you need to comb through all the posts on that particular blog and look for posts that are very closely related to content that you produced on your blog. You're not going to be promoting your blog as a whole on that blog. You're going to be promoting a specific piece of content. This is what makes this blog commenting marketing strategy so powerful. You're focusing on specificity.

Your main pay off is not the direct traffic your blog comment link will generate. While it can generate some traffic, the bigger pay off is when the owner of the blog considers you so authoritative that he or she invites you to post guest materials on that third party blog.

If you get your custom content on all these external third part blogs, you are creating passive pipelines of traffic to your website. Best of all, these are highly-targeted sources of traffic that go to highly-specific pages which increase your chances of converting that traffic into cold hard cash. This is how powerful rifle-shot-highly-target blog commenting can be.

Forum discussions

It's really important to pick forums that have discussions that are tightly related to your niche. Don't just assemble a generic list of forums and create accounts and drop links all over the place, that's going to get you banned and chances are Google might even penalize you if you try to drive traffic that way.

The better approach would be to actively monitor certain high-traffic forums for very specific discussion involving your niche. Just as importantly, make sure that these discussions are tightly related to stuff that you've already written in the past. This way, when you discuss the issues raised in a forum post's reply, when you drop your link, your link actually adds value to what you said. Do you see how this works?

What separates forum spamming from forum marketing is niche specificity and the value your posts add to the existing conversations on the forums you're marketing on.

Reshare on social media

It's really important to understand that since you are creating content that is based on topics that are already hot in your niche, there are already social media accounts talking about these topics. You only need to find these places and reshare your content with them. Since they're already talking about the hot topic that you're focused on and you have a distinct personality-driven spin on the hot topic, chances are high that they would also reshare your content.

This is very powerful because people on social media are not equal. Some people are more influential than others. Some people have more friends than others. If your content truly engages a very popular person, don't be surprised to see a massive burst of traffic because that person shared your blog post on their Facebook wall, Facebook groups, or Twitter feed.

Resharing on social media via related places

Since you've found hot topics via certain social media accounts, and then you reshared with these same accounts featuring your distinct spin, you can take things to the next level. You can find other social media accounts that are similar to those people who are already interested in your content. Similarly, you may find other places where similar content is being shared.

Whatever the case may be, you need to look for places online may they be Facebook Page walls, Facebook groups, Twitter accounts, or YouTube videos that deal with the same type of content you're focused on. Share with these social media accounts. You'd be surprised as to how gladly they would reshare your content.

Make derivative content and share

Once you've created a blog post don't just post, publish, and promote, you can take that same exact content and recycle it into different content forms and share on social media platforms catering to those content forms. To unpack this, let me give you an example.

For example, I created a blog post on baby strollers for my Amazon baby stroller product review site. I then take one of those blog posts and turn them into highly informative slides. Once I have the slides filed through Microsoft Office PowerPoint, I would then take that file and upload it to slide-based media sharing websites like SlideShare.com. Similarly, since I'm dealing with slides, I can share it on Facebook and other social media platforms.

I can also turn my blog posts into PDFs, images featuring a quote from my blog post, I can strip down my blog post into questions and answers, and finally, I can hire a freelancer of micro outsourcing platforms like Fiverr.com and turn my blog post into a narrative video.

Whatever the case may be, I make derivative content from one particular blog post. I then find websites that specialize in sharing that type of content format. In the case of PDFs, I can look for websites like Scribd.com where document uploads are welcome. There are many website that are like Scribd out there.

Similarly, I can take image quotes and upload them to my Facebook fan page and ask my fans to share these quotes on their Facebook walls. Facebook users love sharing quotation pictures. I can then take the question and answer snippets from my blog post and post the questions or the answer on Quora.com or Yahoo Answers. As for the videos, I can use my keyword targets as tags and include they keywords in my description and file names, and upload the videos to YouTube and Vimeo.

There are just so many different social media platforms out there catering to different media types. The key to this strategy is to make derivative versions of the blog post that you have written or your freelance writer has written in the past to create new pieces of content which you can then share.

The strategy is, as long as you can get small drips and drabs of traffic from the dozens, if not hundreds, of shares you've made, this can translate to a nice steady stream of traffic to your blog posts. If you have many blog posts with their own traffic streams, this can add to a nice chunk of traffic.

Chapter 10

Making Money with Blogs is all about conversions

The bottom line to effective blogging is maximizing conversions. You have to remember that for you to make money with your blog, you have to turn that traffic your content is attracting into cold hard cash.

I've already covered monetization models. I've already covered how you should produce content the smart way. I've already covered how to drum up traffic. All that discussion will be useless if you don't have a plan to convert the traffic you attract with your blog.

You might think that conversion is pretty straightforward. You might be thinking that you only need to drum up traffic, get them to your blog post, get them to click an ad, once they clicked on an ad they go to a landing page, and if they buy something you make money. While technically true, there is more to it than that.

You have to think in mathematical terms, so you can make the necessary adjustments to maximize conversions. Otherwise, you're simply left rolling the dice, crossing your fingers, and hoping for the best. Hope is not a strategy.

Pay attention to the following to put together a solid conversion strategy.

How conversions work

The first step in conversion is for users at the places you're promoting on to click on your link. The rate at which they click is your click-through ratio on your links. You need to pay attention to your statistics counter because you would realize that certain traffic sources send more traffic and have better click-through ratios than other traffic sources.

In many cases, a particular traffic source may seem like it's sending you a lot of traffic, but if you look at the actual conversion rate, a traffic source that is sending less traffic might actually be making you more money. You need to pay attention to these patters. This is what I mean by mathematical about your approach to conversions.

You can't just approach this with "the more, the merrier" mindset. That's not going to work. Conversion is all about maximizing your return on effort. This means that for every unit of resources and time you invest in a particular traffic source, you have to get as much dollars in return. Pay attention to the click-through ratio of the different traffic sources.

Next, when the traffic goes to your website, typically, most bloggers' traffic bounces out immediately. They click the back button or they close the window. This is called "bounce". The proportion of people engaging this behavior compared to the overall number of visitors to a page produce your bounce rate.

The higher your bounce rate, the more you should be worried. Unless they're bouncing out by clicking on your ad, you should be worried.

You need people to stay on your pages for as long as possible. Why? You get many bites at the apple. The more they stay on your blog post, the higher the likelihood that you would be branding them and the higher the likelihood that you can convince them to consider your blog knowledgeable, credible, and authoritative in your niche.

This increases the likelihood that they may return. This also increases the likelihood that they may share your content with their friends and family members. At the very least, this also increases the likelihood that they would see more ads and they would click on that ad.

The next step is to make sure that higher dwell times lead to higher on-site CTR. There are two types of CTR or Click-Through Ratio, click-throughs from outside your site and click-throughs within your site. Pay attention to both. You need to pay attention to which popular pages people land on and how they click from those pages to inner pages.

The secret to maximizing conversion is to figure out why your popular pages are popular and make more of them. Interlink them so you can increase your dwell time. When you increase your dwell time, you tend to also increase your on-site CTR.

By maximizing on-site CTR, you also increase conversions. Now, conversions can be tricky because it depends on your monetization model. Pay attention to the specific discussions below.

Increase ad clicks

If you get paid per ad click because you run contextual ad networks like AdSense, for example, you need to increase your ad click volume. The best way to do this is to increase the number of pages on particular visitor would see.

By simply just chopping up otherwise long blocks of texts into small bite size pieces, you can increase the number of pages they view, but this can be very annoying. People don't like jumping through many hoops just to consume content. Chances are very high that they're going to bounce out of your website if you do that.

You have to break up your long posts into long-enough chunks so as to entertain and captivate the reader. Also, each new block that you add to that long chain of pages must add value to the content that they read before. If you do this right, you decrease your bounce rate and increase your dwell time. This can have a positive role as far as your on-site CTR and conversions are concerned.

Increase dwell time

There are many ways to increase dwell time. One of my favorite approaches is to use videos. When people sit down to watch a video, it's a firm decision. Whether that video is three minutes long or thirty minutes long, they are going to be on that page for a long time. This can go a long way in reducing your bounce rate.

The downside to video is the fact that most people are in a hurry. Most people don't have the luxury of time. Posting videos on your blog posts might temporarily boost your bounce rate. However, if the videos are of high quality and the text content on the blog post the video appears with is also high quality, eventually you should develop enough of a loyal user base so that the bounce rate created by the video will decrease.

Eventually, thanks to your loyal blog community, your overall bounce rate can sink quite a bit thanks to the power of video.

Increase CPA/affiliate link conversions

When you increase dwell time and you increase the number of contact opportunities the reader has with your ad materials, you increase the likelihood that they would click-through and enter their ZIP code, email address, or otherwise fill out a survey for CPA forms. Similarly, these practices also increase the likelihood that your visitors would click on an affiliate link.

To maximize CPA and affiliate link conversions, you have to play around with the different ads those offers come with. You might also, if allowed by the affiliate offer, produce your own specific ads that relates specifically to your content.

Whatever the case may be, you need to play around a little bit with your marketing materials for CPA and affiliate link conversions to increase the conversion value of each and every visitor you get to your pages. This is not going to happen overnight. You have to play close attention to your statistics, so you can figure out which approaches work and which don't.

Also, you need to keep an eagle-eye on your overall volume of conversions. Just because you get a lot of ad clicks to a CPA offer doesn't necessarily mean you will be making a lot of money. Focus more on increasing your conversions while maintaining a high level of ad clicks.

Conclusion

As I've mentioned previously, just like with anything else in life, you can always choose to do things the easy way or the hard way. This is definitely true when it comes to blogging. You have to approach your blogging business like a business. You have to pay attention to details. You have to have a solid plan. You always have to have a list of alternative options.

By being both systematic and methodical in approaching blogging, you increase the likelihood that your blog will be a success. You have to apply this results-based and process-driven mindset to all aspects of your blog. Whether you're picking a niche, driving traffic, creating content, or converting traffic into cash, you have to be systematic and methodical about it. Otherwise, it's too easy to waste time, effort, and energy.

Sadly, it's too easy to join the cast majority of blogger who tried and failed at making money online through their blogs.

This book steps you through a concrete strategy formulation process, so you can come up with specific strategies that would work with your own specific set of circumstances. I've consciously shied away from giving you a one-size-fits-all or cookie-cutter "guru" formula. Such approaches rarely work.

Focus instead on going through the process, knowing what to fine-tune, and know what to look out for. This way, you can anticipate issues before they arise and spot opportunities that pop up. I wish you nothing but the greatest success.

Don't miss out!

Visit the website below and you can sign up to receive emails whenever Andres Zamriver publishes a new book. There's no charge and no obligation.

https://books2read.com/r/B-A-AEJE-GQON

BOOKS 2 READ

Connecting independent readers to independent writers.

About the Author

Andres Zamriver, M.A., is passionate Entrepreneur and eCommerce Consultant along with his lovely wife Loly who holds a B.A. in International Business.

Together, they established an online business which they successfully operate in the comfort of their own home (Zamriver Corporation).

To date, Andres has authored an array of books and training courses on all things eCommerce, blogging, online marketing & branding.

His primary mission is creating positive change in people's lives through the power of internet-based entrepreneurship.

During his spare time, you can find him spending quality time with their two beautiful children (Angel & Vicky).

He also enjoys watching soccer games and relaxing at the beach.

Read more at https://6figuresclub.com.

www.ingramcontent.com/pod-product-compliance
Lightning Source LLC
Chambersburg PA
CBHW022116170526
45157CB00004B/1663